Friend

Poems by Young People

Also by Kate Clanchy

Novels
Meeting the English

Poems
Slattern
Samarkand
Newborn
Selected Poems
The Picador Book of Birth Poems (ed.)
England: Poems from a School (ed.)

Non-Fiction
Antigona and Me
Some Kids I Taught and What They Taught Me
How to Grow Your Own Poem

Short Stories
The Not-Dead and the Saved

Friend

Poems by Young People

Edited by Kate Clanchy

Swift

SWIFT PRESS

First published in Great Britain by Swift Press 2023

1 3 5 7 9 8 6 4 2

Copyright © Kate Clanchy 2023
Copyright of each of the poems remains with the poets.

The right of Kate Clanchy to be identified as the Author of this Work has been asserted in accordance with the Copyright, Designs and Patents Act 1988

A CIP catalogue record for this book is available from the British Library

ISBN: 9781800752955
eISBN: 9781800752962

*In memoriam Joan Clanchy (1939–2020),
who gave her life to education.*

Friend,

        Yesterday I saw a dog
that was you, long and rude. It had your short fringe
but didn't wear the clothes you do,
second hand skirts that look like gold on you

and dirt when I borrow them.
Do you remember the days we almost died
together lying in the middle of rural roads,
gravel on the back of our heads?

Do you remember the taste of vegan ice cream
I pretended to like and my conversations
with your mother and brother claiming
I came to Burford just to speak to them and not

to watch you smoke out of your window
listening to 5am owls and laughing till we peed ourselves
while trying not to wake up your grandmother
with our underlying dementia in her. I remember.

I text you how much it hurts not to see you.
Your tattooed legs, your obsession with things
that make me uncomfortable, the £1 sprays
we both smelled of and the ramen we'd make.

Friend, do you miss the words we shared drunk
and upside down, our heads symmetrical, hanging
off the bed? Friend, do you miss the truths we'd tell
each other in churches where I muffled my breath?

I miss the 74 clocks that would tick in the walls
and tock to let us know that the friendship
we ate together would be something
we'd look back to in quarantine.

Aisha Borja (18)

Contents

Introduction xiii

The Life and Times of Bedroom Floor 1

I didn't come from 2

My Dog 3

Bookish 4

Places to Cry 5

Year 7 6

Resolution 7

Tent 8

Friends 9

Mad Bull 10

Eraser 12

Learning English 13

Sham 14

My Spelling 15

Friend 17

Vsst 18

Joke 19

People Pleaser 20

OX4 22

Ode to my Ceiling 23

in between the cracks 24

[*ix*]

My brother 25
Sister 27
Back 28
Aunt 29
Mum, 30
Grief 31
Grandfather 32
Grandma, at least 33
The Place I Once Called Home 34
Wish 35
My Lonely Does Dressage 36
Mingy 37
Silence has its imperfections 38
Lexicon of the Mountain River 39
Full Length Portrait of the Wind 40
Zero 41
Moon 42
Geography 43
The Sea Refuses to be a Sonnet 44
Day Trip 45
Rain 46
I took God with me camping 47
When all this is over 49
To Live 50
For My Future Lover 51

Romance 53

Boars Hill 54

You say nothing ever happens 55

Boys 56

Still 57

Love 58

Icarus 59

Love 60

I love you back 61

Long Distance Relationship 62

Goodbye 63

Sundaes on a Sunday 64

My bed broke up with me 65

Stained 66

The hair you brushed is being cut off 67

I always never wanted to be an adult 68

Equine 69

My heart is a cockroach, caught in the mouth of an alley cat 70

The Most Romantic Thing Ever 71

When I Was a Kid I Waited 72

I've learned to go back 73

Sister 74

My Mother 75

Want 76

My mother tells me she cannot   77
Mother of Flip-flops   78
The Child Under My Ribs   80
Dad   81
Lyndon   82
Mother's Day   84
Ode   86
The Heart in Winter   87
Covering Freud   89
Exam Questions   91
Appointments   92
One of me is writing again   93
My Teacher   95
Grown ups   96
To Do at Uni   98
Today   99
Note   100
What I Miss When I'm Away   101

The Story of this Book   102
Supporting Poetry through this Book   105
The Poets   106
Acknowledgements   114

Introduction

Aisha wrote the poem 'Friend' during a poetry workshop on Zoom during the Covid lockdown of spring 2020. We were all frightened and lonely – that's why I'd gathered my old students in the first place – but as soon as she read out the poem, I was transported to the close bedrooms and reckless feelings of teenage friendship, and so was the rest of the group. The truthfulness and clarity of the poem made us feel less alone.

I started to think of other poems that could do that trick – could keep you company, actually seem to take you into the mind of a teenager. Many of those that came to mind were also by my students, and I thought I would like to group them together. (There is more about how I came to know so many teenage poets, and about the poets themselves, at the end of this book.) So, over the coming months of quarantine, I started to dig out those poems and remind the poets – many grown up now – about them. When they were read as a group, the poems seemed even better; they supplemented and argued with each other, creating something greater than the sum of their parts. It was clear that this was an anthology. And so here, still called *Friend*, it is.

The book begins on a fourteen-year-old's bedroom floor, and ends with a new university student looking back to a similar room. In between, we visit the sea, stand in the rain, grieve, repair, fall in love and out again, and give our families – especially our fathers and mothers – a long, cool stare. None of this is new to poetry, nor is the underlying theme of the book: that youth passes. The difference here is that these poets are not looking back at their experiences from age, but writing as these feelings freshly happen. Their poems have an immediacy and directness that is like talking to a friend. I hope many people, young and old, will enjoy their company.

> Kate Clanchy MBE

The Life and Times of Bedroom Floor

On his floor falls his schoolbag, his tie
and his trainers, his phone with its charger
and three missed calls. On the floor
the detention he may have forgotten to go to.
(His mum's gonna kill him for that.) He lets it all
fall, and him saying this, and her saying that.
He throws down the test he had to redo, the one
that he actually tried on. He puts down
the person he cares so much about.
So much, they'll never know.

His whole world lies on that bedroom floor,
and everyone says it looks like a bomb hit it.

Nell Peto (14)

I didn't come from

the right side of town, warm hands
on the walk to the school, a phone to check
in the middle of class. I didn't know the difference
between *lunch* and *dinner* or *tea* and *supper* or why
a meal was better if it came from the stove not the microwave,
why it mattered if I could figure out the area of a triangle,
    that stealing
was always bad even if you didn't get caught and that
    cigarettes weren't
meant to burn your fingers when you held them

I didn't come from a bedroom all to myself
WiFi that worked past 5pm or clothes that hadn't been
worn before, I didn't know that homework wasn't optional
that you had to say *please* and *thank you* to everyone even if
they were a good for nothing teacher that didn't even
    understand
that sometimes you were late because you had to

wake up your mother and make sure she remembered
to take her tablets and brush her teeth and you had to brush
your own teeth with a toothbrush made for giants that had green
in all the wrong places and tasted like pennies and
    disappointment
and the adverts always said it made everything 'minty fresh' but
the other kids laughed when you spoke

so you stopped speaking altogether.

Maisie Crittenden (19)

My Dog

I talk to my sleeping dog.
I stroke his cold, hard fur
through my fingers. I tell him
the stars are looking out
for everyone at different points
in your life. I tell him my heart
is a rushing lion, a cheetah,
and a cat all running at the same
time but at different speeds.
I tell him people are born
every day, die every day.
I tell him birds squawk
and cats meow. He starts
to twitch his eyes, dreaming
something no human could
possibly live through.
I tell him that my life is a seed,
waiting for water.

Jamie Allport (12)

Bookish

I wanted to be
the Lapland woman's non-existent daughter,
wanted to saddle up the reindeer
with cool practicality.

I wanted to be
Eliza, the sister of the swans,
wanted to stand in that clear pool
in a hidden forest, real.

I wanted to be
the woman in the flowered dress,
wanted to dance with the brother
whose one feathered wing remained.

I wanted to be
Rapunzel's wicked witchy neighbour
with beautiful black hair and a shawl
embroidered with moons and suns.

I wanted to be
Amy March with her pickled limes,
wanted to stand a proud
pretty crosspatch in front of the class.

I wanted to be
a hidden face in the snowy picture book,
wanted to watch the snake in the casket
from the frosted hedge,

wanted to see it bite the children,
wanted to be indifferent.

Helen Woods (12)

Places to Cry

hiding under the apple tree
with the broad branches
and pink flowers;

when feeding the next-door neighbour's fish
blibity blobity blu
halves of food pieces captured;
and taken

underwater;

stuck in the toilet
you know there's a queue
but your pink face tells you to stay;

in your mother's arms
under the shining redcurrant bush
in the pouring rain.

Eva Brand Whitehead (12)

Year 7

I've put my shoulders around my ears,
and I'm sat at the window waiting

for some unidentified flying thing
to appear through a rip in the air

and take me where it's no big deal
if I cross my legs, or there are meerkat stickers

on my lunchbox, or I don't know
at which table to sit or worry, when people

are laughing or where, or whether
their laughter is pointed. I think

I must be an alien. But maybe
that means there are others, somewhere,

a whole alien nation, which I might
glimpse through a telescope. If

I howl at the moon they may not
hear me, so I'll wave through the window,

in the hope that they might see me.
I'll write them a letter, asking

to be beamed up. I might even

        write poetry.

Brennig Davies (20)

Resolution

I will take off my dyslexic coat
and run away in my poetry dress.

I will run a full seven furlongs
with my four magic tigers.

I will hunt down school,
the evil beast that sees me as average.

I will forge a sword
out of my unsettled words.

I will live in a tree until
the wolves of normality run away.

I will let the lark of imagination
out of its iron cage.

I will tame the wildest poems
and lure them into my trap.

And strike them into my page.

Aisha Borja (12)

Tent

If you turn a book upside down
it becomes a tent.
On Wednesdays I crawl inside.
The book smell envelops me like a cloak.
I try to catch the cinnamon dreams
that flit about like butterflies.
Freedom is printed on every page.

Sometimes I stick my head outside
and watch the world turn without a care.
Dad says that if you leave a book
upside down
it breaks its spine.
My spine is broken.

Zola Tatton (12)

Friends

Aisha was a daisy:
an everyday flower that could be a daisy chain;
an embellishment for a hair band;
a sign that summer's coming.

John was a worn-out tarpaulin:
somewhat annoying and it hurts when it hits you;
somehow resilient, endearing, persevering;
kept the rest of us safe and we thanked him for that.

Jim was a toy that got left out in the rain:
a little slow and strange;
a little able to work and play;
a little angry about how he got that way.

Zak was a corner-shop yo-yo
that got stuck a lot and didn't last long.
That was brilliant while it lasted.
That was a treat when it happened.

See you all round.

Nell Peto (13)

Mad Bull

But I don't even need to mention
Monday, Wednesday,
Thursday, Friday, Saturday
and Sunday.
Tuesday is the filled-up bottle,
the others are trash.

And just a year ago we
were jumping through the hoop
pretending to be a mad bull,
which you were.

Seven times we watched that film.
Back to back,
then the sequel came out
and we despised it.
The new crushing the old
like the gravel in the front garden.

Yesterday I saw a book on the shelf
that smiled like you, as if
its yellowed pages
were also full of bouncy words.
I read it in a storm and thought
of the sleepover we made in a den.
You said the midnight feast fairy
would come. We waited hours
till the walls became brick

coated in tissue and sleep
was a kindness, soothing on my face.

But none of that happens now.
My friend, how often do you
gaze at the polaroid pinned
to your cork board. The one
of you cradling my cousin?

I wonder all these things and
other things wander in
robed in purple ink
sprawling all over my page.

Flora Pizey (11)

Eraser

I am what was once white
and is now a dirty ash grey.
In my sides are crudely scratched words:
yes, no, maybe.

I am flipped and twirled through the air
for a child's game, snatched by unasking friends,
coldly catapulted by rulers.

I was made to remove mistakes:
I'm used to raise kingdoms, watch them
be built and destroy them again.
I fear that one day I'll be forgotten.
Rubbed until I'm only a stub.

All I really long for
is stability. A place in the pencil case
where I belong. Me,
not the string of pencils
nor the unnecessary
plastic dinosaur.
What I want is
not to be flung.

Frankie Lee (12)

Learning English

I walk down the road thinking:
don't 'mate' me, mate, don't
make that old-faced mouth
like a squirrel eating
its favourite rubbish
or a bird munching its favourite delicious fly,
making delicious fly noises.

Enormously, obviously, literally . . .
Their favourite word is *actually*.
Mine are *Pardon* and *Excuse Me*.
I feel deaf and dumb.

I want to speak like that.

Timileyin Amusan (17)

Sham

When I was in Syria
I did not count up
how lucky I was
when I raised my hand
to spell the word 'happiness';
when I got each letter correct.

Now my hand is gloved
in strangeness. Now,
I try to write the name
of my country from
the wrong margin.
Four letters. Each letter hurts.

Mohamed Assaf (12)

My Spelling

My spelling is hateful
but I know in many ways
he is more confused than me.

He is young, only eight. Also,
he has PTSD and anger disorder
and addictive personality.

(I have told my spelling
on many occasions not to rip the paper
like banana skins.) My spelling

goes to school in one boot
and one slipper and is never
completely awake. I try

to understand. I remind myself
that really my spelling
just wants to fit in. He tries

to sing like all the other children
but it comes out all out of key
and much too loud. My spelling

has glasses but one lens is missing
and he forgot them, anyway.
My spelling loves papers and pens.

He hopes that one day
he will wave the words around
like everyone else.

Aisha Borja (14)

Friend

Let's doodle round the holes in our paper
and tap patterns into the silence.
I want to tell you the story
of why we should get a round of applause
for smiling
when it doesn't go with our outfits
or your slappable face.
You make me want to condition your hair
at 1.22am.
You make me want to run through trains
and whistle with braces and pick up the sun,
pat it dry, and hand it to you.
I've never not worried about you,
the way fears won't stain your orange peel cheeks
scares me.
You make me want to smell
the miscellaneous clouds
in the weight of the words you gave me.

Edie Michael (14)

Vsst

say the watered-down teenagers
with baggy tracksuits
carrying the weight of the world
in their pockets, clutching
their knife-shaped teddies
that will never taste blood.
3 stripes run down their bodies
like the wax in their hair.
Their snapped-back caps
hold up delicate figures
filled with stressful failures.
Vsst they all say
shrugging their heavy shoulders
burrowing their hands
into something-filled pockets.

Toby Stephenson (14)

Joke

Their noise echoes, the voices with no depth, they run in circles, the voices of the boys who ignore me, the boys who always fit in, the boys who think I'm a weirdo, the ones I shout at and all they do is laugh. The boys who play a constant game of football, kicking the small sphere against the solid walls of my head where it shatters my thoughts and all they do is laugh. The boys who speak in one voice; who chant YouTube videos, the ones which don't even make sense; the boys who are empty but fill up with voices; the boys who think sexist thoughts that only cowardice keeps in: for they are the boys who laugh, and I am the girl who humours them.

Zola Tatton (11)

People Pleaser

This is how to listen
but only hear white noise.
This is how you structure a PEE paragraph
so you seem civilised.

This is how to stand tall
so that you're not as low
as your self-esteem.
This is how to sit upright

so you don't hurt her pride.
This is how to lose weight to finally wear
that dress she bought you in size 8.
This is how you later hang

that same top up to avoid a debate
about how you'll attract
negative attention and get in a state
and it'll be too late.

This is how you scrub
the kitchen surface squeaky clean.
Don't do a half job.
Don't make a scene.

This is how you write a poem
for the chapters of life
you don't read aloud. This is how
you accept a compliment: with a smile

you don't believe in.
This is how you sew a sleeve.
And this is how to close your eyes.
This is how you breathe.

Iesha Jennings (15)

OX4

On average people in OX4 live 15 years fewer than those in OX1

OX4 is the dirt under fingernails,
OX4 is curry leaves sleeping on the edge of my plate,
4 is soft turmeric fingerprints tattooed down your stairs.
I watch you roll 4 up in tight Rizla hugs.
OX1 watches OX4 smash a window
with a mud-caked football, photographs
the glass shards perched on moss-embroidered concrete,
will never understand that in OX4 'I can imagine
you as a doctor' isn't a compliment.
OX4 writes chalky words that get brushed off
the smooth cream paint, the kind of chalk
that makes you cough if you breathe it in too deep.
But all 4's words are stained anyway. The 4 stain
won't wash out. Today the news is orange:
so many people ill with 4. I take 4 into myself,
hate my middle name, Charvi. It means
'good with words', but to 1 it means 4.
4 doesn't walk on the pavement. 4
runs in the road. 4 is the plaster that stripes my skin
like mismatched floorboards, 4 is salted streaks
down hot brown cheeks, 4 is the sun
slipping behind clouds. A loss of possibility.
A broken zip.

Anna Beekmayer (17)

Ode to my Ceiling

Your glow is faint and luminous.
Your planet stickers are stuck for eternity.
I look up to you when there is nothing else.
You make me disassociate
from the reality of being alone.
Those planets staring at me like eyes –
I'm not alone right now.

The ceiling isn't either.

Joanna Champion (15)

in between the cracks

in the ceiling
my breaths float and flit about
with the whispers that Jenny sent to Alice
with the thoughts that slip
through my fingers
the words I forgot
how to write.

I think if
I concentrated hard
enough on those jagged
jittery cracks I could sit
in that gap in the ceiling
with the thoughts
and the whispers
and myself.

Zola Tatton (12)

My brother

Your body
Is two dimensional, a stick man's
Your head
Is a graphite-rimmed circle in a children's exercise book
Your eyes
Are portholes to the places where your soft toys live
Your scar just above your right eye
Is my regret. (I should have moved the desk with sharp
   edges away)
Your nose
Is the graceful curve of a crescent moon
Your breath
Is a warm version of the most recent snack
I have given you: wagon wheels, orange smiles,
crisps, grapes, chocolate spread sandwiches
Your mouth
Reads out lines of the play I have to learn so I can act out
   my part
Your anger
Is the flame of a tea candle for me to pinch with two fingers
Your ribs
Are a xylophone
Your back
Is a chain of pearls
Your hands
Are goalkeeper's gloves flattened in a sweaty sports bag
Your toes
Are piggies which go to market

True to your name, Peter,
Your body is my rock and I
am the tide which always comes back to you.

Naomi Rae (18)

Sister

And when we were young
we used to fight till the day was up,
And when midnight struck
and our eyes closed we always said, *I love you* . . .

And when the nurses told us
Dad wasn't progressing
we sat down on a wall near Waterloo Bridge,
and when the piper was playing 'Amazing Grace'
you whispered *I will always be here even if our father won't.*
And when you moved,
and I had to learn to live without you –

It was like my shadow leaving as the light enters.

Hollie Peterson (16)

Back

Our dear aunt she has gone back again,
and lo! We are here, back in the hospital
where the corridors are long and slopey so
unconsciously you too are set into the rolling mood,
where time isn't quite ticking and you mould
into the soft garments and tissue around you.
Here the walls are all the same pale pea green,
that supposedly calming colour though
you tend to feel in fact this long corridor
is under the sea and winding you in deeper,

to where our dear aunt has a rug wrapped
round her legs so she looks like a mermaid
floating in the green sea. We remember
she has been here many times before, and
has always returned home. Always. But
somehow it happens that we return here
to the low green corridors, the soft garments,
the supposedly calming colour green as if
mermaids could only live in this sea.

Linnet Drury (11)

Aunt

I can still hear your feet going back and forth,
doing the job of two people,
so you could put a meal on the table.

I can still see you dragging your kids to school
so they didn't have your life.
You never sat down to eat the fruit of your labour.

When you pushed sweet things down your throat
I saw your eyes shouting for help.
I saw your mouth not listening.

I can still feel your pain after you withered,
wanting to be there for your kids
wishing your mouth had listened, had cried out for help.

Flower. It still hurts that I couldn't water you.

Timileyin Amusan (19)

Mum,

You're a candle
with a burned-down
flame, with wax melting
down its edges. You're a
mystery box full of problems
and questions which have never
been answered. You were always
there when I needed comforting. I
was never there when your eyes filled
and tears streamed like swirling rivers down
your wrinkled face. I wish I could go back
in time so I could see you again. See your
smile. Smell your perfume which still
tickles my nose. You're the sunset
I watch when I walk back
from school. You're the
elephants in my room
which still smell of
your perfume.

Ghost.

Hollie Peterson (15)

Grief

When the computer shoots the printer
and deletes the whole folder
we write grief.

When the death has already happened
yet your great grandma still sits in her chair,
that is grief.

When words twist into one another creating a song
that explodes in your eyes,
that's grief.

And in the blackberry bushes where we hid
our love for one another,
grief also sits,

holding a sphere and wearing a crown of thorns,
letting the blood roll over his torn head.
Grief is also

in the hospice next to your cousin, knitting
a hat for her moon head, and when
she dies grief sleeps

under your aunt's bed.

Aisha Borja (16)

Grandfather

Today, I imagined you during Art.
Did you really have to leave
just then? Four years ago now.
I'm sorry and sad that you did.

You're a huge creative mountain
that I don't remember, just
a 'whack' playing tennis on a summer
day and eating ice cream in the sun.

I miss not getting to know you better.
I miss not spending these years
with you. I miss the memories of you
I didn't get to make.

William Harrison (11)

Grandma, at least

you weren't there when the roof caved in
just one week later and the boiler
spewed golden insulation everywhere

like dragon sick. Or for the asbestos.
Or lockdown. And it's lucky
I took the precious photos from out

the drawer that would later
bulge and explode under the weight
of the damage. I just had a feeling. Like how

when I left you *just for a few days* and though
the district nurse said it would be fine, I said
goodbye as if I meant it, and it was.

Linnet Drury (17)

The Place I Once Called Home

Come out say my friends
and little do they know
how much I wish I could.
But: *No*, I say and I switch

my phone off. When I arrive
nothing is the same. My bunkbed
and wardrobe are smaller than me,
my accessories are in the same jar

I left them. My worries hover
over me like a bunch of birds
on a piece of bread. So I drop
the key ring and walk out, breathe

in the cold polluted air. Tears
stream down my face because
the accessories are still
in their place, safe, but my life

has a missing piece
from its puzzle and can never
be completed again because
my mother is dead.

Hollie Peterson (16)

Wish

(for my father)

I wish I could give you a present
instead of always flowers,
capture Saturdays in snapshots.
hugs in the blink of an eye,
wrap a box up in purple and blue,
and send it all to you.

I wish I could send you a present.
I'm fed up with flowers.
And put in that photo of you
where you're smiling your smile
and balancing on rocks.
And your eyes are alive. Alive.

If I could send you a present,
Dad, I wouldn't give you flowers.
I'd string a box to a balloon,
let it float on up to you.
And in the corner of the box
I'd put my love and tie it up –

and kiss it all goodbye.

Rhianna Graham (16)

My Lonely Does Dressage

He bought me my lonely for Christmas
Because it seems I asked for it.
And it turned out to be non-returnable,
though I begged for the receipt.

I'd have cried a while beside the tree.
but I couldn't find the energy.
So I went online, and spent two hours
buying items for my lonely.

A stable for it to sleep in,
some hay for it to eat,
a bar so it could show-jump;
steel shoes to fit its feet.

Now my lonely does dressage.
I ride on its back in the pen.
And we go round and round in circles
until it feels like December again.

Brennig Davies (20)

Mingy

Is the longing for the next season to return
so you can wish for the next season to that. Usually,
it's celebrated on a Sunday. The second Sunday
of a January. For the full experience, shut

yourself off, lock your door, look at the words
in a book and feel your shoulders sink
into your mingy bed, listen to the mingy rain
and deal with the mingy struggle of reading

a book while lying down. Breathe in the mingy
wet light. Make a game out of catching
your warm, mingy tears on the end of your nose,
and pretend you are ok.

Edie Michael (14)

Silence has its imperfections

The way it wants to run away
through the yellow rapeseed fields
and tell you all its secrets

how it gets sick of being ignored
and shoved into a corner
of feeling invisible,

of coming out at night
only to be interrupted by
drunken yells

of never being embraced,
of being hated
for smelling of exams.

It does not protest.
But then silence could never talk.
Only weep.

Maddie Wolf (14)

Lexicon of the Mountain River

Fforersan (fo-se-ran)
The cry of a wolf whose baby is gone

Shodaw (show-dau)
The spirit which follows an individual after a great
   loss or grief

Heielant (hi-lang)
Being left with laughter

Selsoic: (sell-stow-is)
When sadness is eclipsed by hope

Ingle lacht (ing-legl lac-h)
Golden laughter/sunlight smile

Zum lgggeims (sun gloom)
Lit: filled with gold. To begin again with hope.

Frankie Lee (12)

Full Length Portrait of the Wind

She wants to leave the city.
The tower blocks stop
like flocks of sheep in the road
and her hair is full of scrap metal
and her teeth have tower block windows
and her eyes are empty coal mines
and her tarmac hands are crossed
with double yellow lines
that the fortune-teller couldn't understand.
Her tongue is sharp and electric as a telephone wire.

She missed the train again
and so she spins in a despairing merry-go-round
of dizzy aerials and left-hand gloves
and disembowelled plastic bags.
Her shoe soles are a patchwork of roof tiles.
Pigeons hang from them like bats.
Sometimes she might press her broken-bottle eyes
to your window
but you will be too busy saying
how the wind is howling like a wolf around your house
to notice.

If you looked up you might see
the tunnel of her pupil with cat's-eye lights
to mark the way.
She sighs, pointedly, down your chimney.
She was only on her way to catch the train.

Helen Woods (14)

Zero

This was going to be a metaphor
for emptiness but anyone who starts writing
a poem about maths is confused in some way
and at the moment I am as hollow as a shell
in a sea without a shore, a book
still wrapped in clingfilm, a child
who can only sing in the minor key, an anomaly maths error an

extra

in an animated film in which I take the place
of grout. Expanding foam, and nozzle

of a glue gun. The other night I was thinking
about why winter doesn't mean as much
as spring, why some people don't laugh
at all. Why such empty things as

shells can sing like the sea. Who appeals
to the major key. Tomorrow
I will be the absence of the absence of
everything. An
anti-zero.

Linnet Drury (14)

Moon

I want to be the moon
and not in Year 11. I want
to be admired for who I am
and not for the box you fit me in.
I want to be the moon, so I can
fade away when you're speaking.
I want to be endless and infinite.
Everywhere – not stationary for hours
on end. I would like to be invisible,
forgotten with the seasons.

You with your *a squared plus
b squared equals c squared,*
your *aller, être,* your infinitives
and ongoing dictatorships.
Don't try to speak to me, because
I'm slipping out of here.
Don't gaze at me in awe
when you looked through me before.
I am going to be the moon,
and you won't recognise me.

Iesha Jennings (15)

Geography

We were meant to get
hard data but
our experiment was eaten.
A seagull picked it
out the water
and took it to a groyne.
Rap tap tapped
it, our apple.
Two
red cheeks ripped
apart like a confession
of miscomprehension.
We would never record
the rate of flow
of longshore drift.

Our boots spent
the uneaten hours building
up a collection
of bitty stones and
sand to walk home in.

Linnet Drury (14)

The Sea Refuses to be a Sonnet

In daytime the sea is in love with the sky; each wave
Is reaching out to touch its blue-grey face
The sea smooths gold in a blink and leaves it cold
On the sand as a piece of twisted wood.
The sea eats the ugliness of aeroplanes
And spits out gannets, albatrosses, gulls
The sea reads the words written on the beach
And sings them to the sky, who rains them down
On the rolling waves in high disdain.
At night the sea blows breath of fire and lights
The yellow moon, then eats its supper off it.
It cries over life and the living, embraces the dead.
No poet can tame it; it will not be a sonnet.

Helen Woods (12)

Day Trip

Nature is surprisingly loud. As I watch
the tearful surface of the lake
make the trees spin, the wind
and the trills and squawks
rival our voices.

The pores of the ground
are like yellow faces, and
silhouette me when I hover
straight above.

The rotting branches are green.
Moss is curling hair.
Mud is swallowing up my legs,
caressing and sinking.
I can't pull them out.

The sky is broken. I don't look up
to see it, for the ground slips down
away, but the white glass
is smashed. Black branches thread out
jagged shapes, the bird nest
where the hammer hit it.

Jasmine Burgess (17)

Rain

I'm abused by the way it stops me.
People hide in corners,
run away from the criminal
the police never arrest.

Timileyin Amusan (17)

I took God with me camping

Here God – this is a tent. It leaks.
Round raindrops soak our bedclothes
and we wake with wet toes. This
is my dominant friend ordering
the tent poles when she doesn't know
what she is doing. You made her, God.
These are my wellies. Thank you
for the gift of these and for the provision
of money to buy them. When I camp,
they are (dare I say it) a God-send.
God, these are portaloos. They are crap.
Yesterday's grass stains, mud clumps
and only you know what else, litter
the hollow floor. God, this is a zip.
It was the only thing standing between
a thief and the contents of my purse.
Here is my dominant friend declaring,
hands on hips, she knows who did it,
but who has no more clue than the rest of us
penniless sods staring at open suitcases.
But someone did it, God. They are one
of six thousand on this campsite,
spending my change on doughnuts and coke.
The Prodigal Son springs to mind, but God,
that lesson is one of the hardest to learn.
Besides, forgiveness is not one of the Ten
Commandments and Thou Shalt Not Steal
is number eight. God, I know you didn't make

our tent, the loos or zips, but why did you make
all this rain? Even my dominant friend
calls on you God, when she sees the state
of the sky. But now it is eleven pm
and the dark that you called night. This
is a thermos flask: hot chocolate – would you
like to taste? This is a woolly hat, a hoody,
wellies that I haven't removed since
Thursday. These are four folding chairs,
arranged in a circle. And above us, God,
are all your stars.

Esme Partridge (16)

When all this is over

I'm going to run till the end of the beach in Aberdyfi,
Till it turns into the beach in Tywyn,
Till it turns into the Promenade,
Till it turns into the rocks leaning into the sea.
When all this is over, I won't turn back.

The damp air will drizzle in through my panting breath:
slight sharp pain each time. The immeasurable white mist
won't let me see if I could jump over the rocks.
I will untie my laces with numb sweaty fingers,
Peel off my sharp scented socks. My soles will feel
the edge of the earth's smooth firmness.
When all this is over, I'm going to jump in
swoop down into the darkness, stretch
my arms to their full span no walls to push against,
run the gritty sea floor against my fingers
I want a jellyfish to sting me.

Do you remember when my only fear was their sting?
You had to lift me above each new wave.
I'm not afraid of them now.

Throw me in.

Naomi Rae (18)

To Live

I want a frisbee for slicing
an empty park, opened windows
for an angry wind,
a bike for a backwards hill.

Give me a race I will
lose, a joke I will finish. I want
a busy room to sink in, rows
of real teeth under a real ceiling.

The future can go fuck itself:
to hell with checkboxes
pressed against pens, to hell with
Leave meeting?

Just tell me stories with your
skateboard as our bench – give us
a day of abandoned car parks
and gritty spit on kerbs,

then a moonlit walk to the corner
shop along double yellowed
streets to buy 2 Fantas and a packet
of salt and vinegar crisps.

Annie Davison (17)

For My Future Lover

Sometimes it feels like indigestion,
Sometimes like gut-wrenching cramp.
Sometimes I want to call you and say
Here's my pain. Understand me.
It takes everything in me to wait for you.

Sometimes I want to know what it is about me you love,
so that I can admire it on your behalf.
Do you think about my hair, my hips, my heart?
(Sometimes the pillow swallows my tears.)
I would give you all of these things in the lace
of my fingers through yours.

Sometimes I want to know the curved pearl
of your ear, the slope of your nose, the habits
of your shoulder blades —
so I can have a piece of you to keep me going.

In my dreams you are real as my bed sheets, solid
and hot. Then I wake and sit up, listening
to the rain in the pipes and
missing you.

Sometime I will write —
I've fallen for you — hard as the bottom of a well.
You scare the elbows off my arms; you have some power.
It takes a lot of boy to scare me.

Sometime I will say – *Just*
drop by when you're next in town, I'll be waiting.
We can eat ice cream in the meadow
and sit by the fire reading poetry aloud.

Lover, I am sitting on my bed, at 00.57,
the lamp light glints
off my pen and I'm
planning our beginnings.

I do all these things,
on my own,
missing you.

Esme Partridge (16)

Romance

Instead of these bored rooms what if
we were in Italy. Rome. In a cafe tourists know

as a home away from home, slipping in
and out of coffee 18-year-olds drink

when the world tells them they're old enough
and pretend we're not looking

at the boys on the table behind you. In Italy
we'd laugh with our disgusting laughs about

how we met, and the time you, and when I,
and what we wore that day. Your hair

would swim around your neck making you
a model and the skin you once told me

you hated would glow and I would join
the long line of men in love with you.

Aisha Borja (18)

Boars Hill

Come with me to Boars Hill,
where the land peaks and troughs
like the tide slamming the beach
the froth of the sea dotting the ocean
like the blossom trees on the land

Come with me to Boars Hill. We can make
daisy lanterns, collect rabbit skulls
and dried leaves, take them back to my room
and arrange them on my ceiling;
a mural dedicated to days we have lost.

Come with me to Boars Hill. I want us
to compare each other's hands
and touch each other until we fall asleep,
and the sun scorches our skin. I never
thought I'd miss touch this much.

Amber Frizzell (17)

You say nothing ever happens

But lie on your back and watch
a menagerie of clouds trot by,
and the birds, with their building societies,
the small ants, in the tall grass, with theirs.

A baby cries, somewhere far away,
and the mother speaks French as she soothes it.
Somewhere there's a man in a Coke bottle factory
watching as the lids get screwed on.

And it's stroganoff for dinner,
and my post got 13 likes,
and I'm starting to think that I love you,

but you'd have to look closely to see.

Brennig Davies (20)

Boys

the black hole at the beginning of time
is the sweat soaking through our thin white tees
the open mouth at our armpits asking:

Oh don't we stink of running
Oh don't we stink of crushed nocturnal insects
Oh don't we stink of moonlight whipped across our faces
Oh don't we stink of dripping mango sorbet
sticking down our words

Mukahang Limbu (17)

Still

I think the wind is coming out my body slowly
everything is like a movie fix
slowly gently in my eyes
the people are leaving
and I find colours of love
in clothes and wool –

I can find love.

Timileyin Amusan (17)

Love

You make me into bubbling water,
spitting and gasping. I swing
round the trunk of a tree
and whisper. I boil over
and out of my eyes.

You make me into a light beam,
which must go at light speed,
and time stops at that speed. I travel 13
billion light years in an instant. I can't stop
till the universe collapses.

You make me into a balloon
I expand. Blow up. But a single word
is a needle. I prickle. I detonate
into small plastic shreds.

Jasmine Burgess (15)

Icarus

My love for you
is clouded by laughter
and midnight
and balloons.

Together we will fly
and if we end up too close to the sun
we will catch each other
and fall as one body.
We are no tale of Icarus:

he who flew alone and
didn't stop
to hold hands
or eat jelly
or admire the light from afar.

Nymph Carter (14)

Love

There should be a word for
the sound when we
speak at the same
time
and the letters chink against
each other,
spilling the wine that was in
the glasses.

There should be a word for the word
that never forms,
the sounds that don't
echo and
the syllables that are
stuck together with bad glue.
But there isn't.
So
I love you
will have to do.

Flora Pizey (13)

I love you back

                        with all the stick
sticky words we heard in the cinema that night.

Your light has made imprints
on the backs of my eyelids.

I could stare at you like the moon
stares at the sun: forever, blind.

The time you held my hand
is the only time I felt full and safe.

Where your arm was
is round my waist like smoke.

Aisha Borja (15)

Long Distance Relationship

Stay. I'm here sat on our swing,
phone clasped in hand. You'll pick up
this time. The curling rubber cord
stretched out as you leave. And leave.
Your phone zipped in the pocket
of your coat as you walk far
away. Sometime you'll pick up when
the cord is so tense. And you'll speak
Can't talk now. You're far from me, too far.
Through the woods
the blue curling line is twisted
around twigs and forgotten.
But I haven't.

Ellie Steel (14)

Goodbye

We are picking our way to the river. The ground crunches
and lifts us like a drum. Vibration. Sound.
My shivers are so solid they could make music.

This is a coldness we can eat together.
It is inside my guts. I don't know if
there are tears pearling down my face, or yours,

and someone must be half-wolf and howling,
because how else could the air shake so much?
This is a place where letters don't make words.

I crouch and my hands find the river.
You, splashing water on your face,
are part of me, here.

This is telepathy. Emitting emotion
and receiving it, energy crackling and jumping
between two bits of wire.

I mouth *Goodbye*.
The water flows on, relentless.
And the trees hiss
through the wind.

Jasmine Burgess (15)

Sundaes on a Sunday

I was at an ice-cream parlour with
my two best friends ordering energy
drink ice cream with a scoop of
kinder bueno and my friend had a waffle
with peanut butter and m&ms and
ate my ice cream too. We spoke
about gossip, who cheated on who,

who cried last lesson on Friday. It was
raining and I could hear the drops
loud and clear but not louder than
the gossip and everything was normal.
I was just a teenage girl in an ice-cream parlour
with her two best friends. A girl who had

had something taken from her an hour before.

Amber Day (16)

My bed broke up with me

My bed spat me out.
Now I'm walking like a year-old child

learning his first steps, mouth wide open
calling for food, pushing out lots
of carbon dioxide.

Now I'm staring at myself like a stranger
listening to silent noises vibrating
through my eardrum.

Bed. The same bed that last night
wanted my love and hugs.
The bed I pushed away.

Now morning smells like fresh coffee
when the kitchen is miles away.

Timileyin Amusan (17)

Stained

Even my finest dress is stained with you,
tainted with your fingertips touch.
I cannot wear her.
She hangs limp in my closet alone.
I want her better,
though I don't want to
wash the dress:
The soap will surely make it clean.
Pure. And new.
Not you.

Ellie Steel (15)

The hair you brushed is being cut off

It shivers as it gushes through
your pink comb
as it tries to remember your dappled eyes
to remember your circumspect fingernails

my hair is a field looked upon from a hill

cold scissors run circles around my neck
like the feeling when you smile

my hair is goat-like in its crease line you said

my hair hides in my mother's childhood
it watches Maisy on the computer in the cupboard
it tries to remember the constellation of your freckles,

as it clings to the kitchen floor.

Eva Brand Whitehead (16)

I always never wanted to be an adult

I want to tell you the story
of when the tree fell over the stream
and I crossed over it to a new place,
a forest. You make me want
to be younger again, to be careless
again. To be able to cross that tree
without breaking it and falling in.

I don't know what it means to leave
the forest behind, to enter
the dull world of consistency.
I don't know what it means now
I keep counting down to the end
when before I was counting up
to the end of my childhood.

You make me almost want
to end this life to see
if it will start again.
When life is handed to us on a plate
we eat it up
but when we cook it ourselves
we only burn it.

Alex Dunn (14)

Equine

I won't pretend to be a person.
I'm a paddock of horses in a trench coat;
that's the reason I bite.

Not a boy, but a braying; not a man,
but a stamping of hooves, and a dark, wet
smell; a canter decanted into the shape of
a child who was a pleasure to teach.

I won't pretend to be a person
when I'm just the urge for running; a tangle,
wedded to being unbridled; a bag
of unsaddled bones that cannot find a stable

and cannot decide if it wants one.

Brennig Davies (20)

My heart is a cockroach, caught in the mouth of an alley cat

This cat has not always been feral. It had known
the warm spot on the rug in front
of the fireplace. But on a summer's day someone
left the door open. The cat, not knowing
any dark thing, leapt away from love. (My heart
leaves open cans of sardines for the alley cat.
Even runaways full of regret deserve to be fed.)
The cat makes a bed of missing pet posters
the wind tore down.
And the cat is hissing at shadows in its sleep.
And the cat is shivering in its matted fur.
And the cat is meowing at the restaurant backdoor.
A waiter, who is also my heart, leaves the backdoor open.
So the cat can be warm for the rest of his shift.
But the cat is feral. The owner of the restaurant
shoves him back into the snow with a broom.
The cat sleeps until the snow reminds it of the rug.
Small things seem sadder when they are alone.
So the cockroach does not mind being in the jaw
of something just as lonely. A little girl
follows the paw prints that made a snow angel
around the cat. Despite the cockroach
in its mouth and its matted fur she picks it up.
And the cat, who knows of dark things now,
spends summer in the lap of the little girl
who is also my heart.

Kyla Pereles (17)

The Most Romantic Thing Ever

Once, two sparrows got trapped
inside a mine. The miners threw down crumbs
and they thrived in the perfect dark,
until there was a family, a flock,
who couldn't see each other
and could barely fly
and knew nobody else.

Jasmine Burgess (17)

When I Was a Kid I Waited

for my dad to come through the door.
Someone I had never seen before.
Waited for a call to come on the phone.
Instead I sat there all alone.

On Father's Day he didn't come,
didn't get in contact with my mum.
I've never seen him, never, no.
He's never been here, never shown.

Maybe I'll never see him, ever,
like some everlasting vendetta.
Maybe my life could have been better.
Not even a call. Not one letter.

Louie Wright (15)

I've learned to go back

To go back to the messed-up kitchen,
the smashed bowls and plates.

To go back to my mum's broken nose
and ripped ear.

To go back there and wait, watching it happen,
knowing there is nothing I can do.

To go back to when I screamed
at my father to stop, to make things worse.

To back even to when a glass bowl smashed on my face,
leaving permanent marks.

I go back to the last day the abuse will happen.
To when it all went quiet.

Amber Day (15)

Sister

I still have your jumper
from when you came up to the hospital.
And we are very different
but also kind of similar
and it hurts that you don't talk to me
and I don't talk to you either,
and I still have the bracelet you gave me,
and it's too big for my wrist but I look after it
like a bone in my body. You saved my life,
and I'll wear your fluffy jumper again

and live a little.

Joanna Champion (15)

My Mother

Is the corridor between two rooms
at 1pm.

She's the clink of mugs
gathered in fours.

She sounds like
thread
snapping between teeth
with some thread
still in your mouth.

My mother's eyes
are the sunset at 16:00
staining your living room
pink.

My mother
will always
be a language
I'll never understand.

Amaani Khan (17)

Want

Want is quiet but it sticks around.
It takes a seat before it makes itself known.
Want's eyes glint, and its tongue flickers.
Want will listen, and wait, and study,
it learns everything. It learns you.

Want smiles and soon after it laughs –
not with you.
Want mocks in whispers and sometimes
(if you are unlucky)
want will shout.

Rachel Gittens (16)

My mother tells me she cannot

wash clothes on a Tuesday.
She tells me it's bad luck.

I wonder if Tuesday was the day
my mum went to the post box

to mail a letter to her family
in Pakistan about life in Britain

but ended up going home and leaving it
in her top drawer, sealed. I wonder

what could have happened if
my grandmother had been the sort

to wash clothes on a Tuesday, to tell
her daughter to make her own luck.

Amaani Khan (17)

Mother of Flip-flops

For my mother, Rina

Mother of flip-flops, of
chipped nail polish on ginger fingers — always
the warm hands, your smile
the kindest room in this house where
we kill cockroaches with bay leaf
you cook in your chai.

Mother of the money-plant, of orchids
you cannot take care of, of the garden
full of weeds only you
can't seem to stand, mother
of turning the light on, the switch clicks
like your broken English when you say

Fill this form, look up this apartment —
What this email say? And maybe
I'll reply to the lady who works at
the bank writing about your loan and
put it in the pre-paid envelope but
maybe I won't. Maybe

I'll send for a loan renewal, a debt
rescindment, address another chance for you
to go to school, learn to hate
fractions, cook words out of alphabets
like rice cakes, to go flirt, to ride
on the back of some handsome's bike,

to keep dancing, to never be pregnant, to learn
to make curry later in life, for yourself
not for some stranger's in-laws. Mother
I'll ask for some dirt for your knees
those black knees of playing

too late in the streets –

Mukahang Limbu (18)

The Child Under My Ribs

She was one of so many. The quiet
middle good one, with nails bitten down
till blood drew, and a Willy Wonka haircut.

She sits under my ribs and remembers
the drunk lady sat on the pavement
at that one corner between mosque and home

shouted *You dirty pakis, fuck off now*
to my sweet five foot no inches mother
who would place herself between all seven

of us children and the lady, or the man
or the dog, or whoever it was who wanted
to swear at us on each day of the week.

The child can't forget her helpless thoughts.
What would she do if someone hit her Ammi?
Would she scream for help? Would she fight?

Could she? Powerless and vulnerable, she clutches
a handful of hijab in chubby fingers, watches
sixteen little legs hurry faster and faster home.

Today that child eases past my ribs, flows
through my fingertips and hugs my mum,
a little tighter, a little longer.

Asima Qayyum

Dad

Your doodles and your imagination.
Your wanting to do more, maybe too much
and never taking no for an answer.
Your wanting to help when you shouldn't;
when you don't need to. The amount
you have taught me. It surprises me. I like that.

William Harrison (11)

Lyndon

This cat looks like you,
which sounds mean, but isn't meant to be —
the way it sits on the pavement, watching,
so weary of cars and dogs.

And this squirrel looks like you,
which sounds strange, because it is —
you told me once they're lucky,
though you don't believe in luck.

And this sweater looks like you,
though I never saw you wear it.
But it's yours, and I wear it
because it's blue, and
because it's yours.

How are you? And how is work?
And were you lonely when you went to Japan?
Sat on the plane by yourself;
asking strangers to take your picture.

When I was sad, you said you'd been sad,
though not in so many words:
a council house by the mountains,
a walk to the gym in the mornings.

And now I make my own breakfasts,
and iron my own clothes,
and realise how much you said
in not so many words,

like the exes you don't end your texts with,
but I've learnt to read anyway.

Brennig Davies (20)

Mother's Day

She glares, she growls from across
the room, feet up on the sofa, reading
the blurb of a book on Mother's Day.
She's on a roll, two arguments in already.
The evening is sulking. My sister
and her incense are in the kitchen making
a friend's recipe, headphones on so high
she can't hear me or herself but can watch
reflections dance in the windows that become
mirrors after dark. She's sieving flour into
a bowl in a rhythm. By her feet the baby
of the house, our cat, waits. She's pregnant,
like this house, belly like a water balloon.
We can all agree motherhood doesn't fit
something that's barely a year old though
my great grandma birthed her first child
at 13. Her childhood soaked into the thing
she cradled and into the wedding photos that
look like me dressing up as a princess
in pre-school, holding a plastic baby, getting
married with Haribo rings. My Year 6 puberty
lessons and the egg baby I had to carry
are blessings, I think, they are the beads
my great-great-grandma counts on her rosary.
For *Jesus y mi abuela Teresa*, who is probably
sitting in a rocking chair in the most populated
house I know surrounded by great aunts,
content. I look up at my own mum.

My sister puts a tray in the oven and shuts it
with her hip. These evenings, let me be grateful
for the beings who care for the fragile
so I am able to grow and make my own
mistakes. I raise a toast to my mother
who has just started re-reading *Love in a Time
of Cholera*, light over her shoulder
imprinting a shadow on the wall behind her
like a halo.

Aisha Borja (17)

Ode

Sherbet lemons, marigolds, sweet tea – why
Are there never enough velvet words for them?
It is thought that to speak of peanut butter
And the clatter of spoons in a drawer of receipts
Is unfathomable. Not to me. I could natter
Of their glory all evening. I could talk about
Bubble baths, and magpies, and your heart

Of course, hung up there on a coat hanger –

Nymph Carter (14)

The Heart in Winter

My heart
the square tiles of frost on the roof, their melting
as I walk to school, the white sunrise like scattered ash.

My heart,
grey knuckles wrinkling, fingers shedding snake skin.
My heart, the brown leaves felted into tarmac, stick

-ing to my boots,
the sound of ripping them off, the cold
searching in the morning for socks. My love

lit
by an electric lamp like my homework, lit by the row
of lamps home, love coming slow like expected rain, shivering

like me outside,
holding my pencil case like chattering teeth. Look, heart,
murmurations like the sky has been shot by a machine gun.

My heart
the dodgy Yale lock and my skin stuck to the key
like spider silk, Love waits outside. Love like November, like

how food
takes longer to cook. My heart pouring out my eyes
at the first sunset I've seen for three weeks –

the row of trees over the hill like toy soldiers, like a row
of matches,   heart,
like set on fire.

Linnet Drury (17)

Covering Freud

My psychology teacher is covering Freud.
A different boy laughs each time Oedipus
is mentioned but when it's Electra,
all the girls stay quiet. We self-administer

ink blot tests. The boys see wolves and men
carrying axes. The girls find butterflies
and women asleep on couches. My teacher says
this all means sex, the duality of it. My teacher says

Freud diagnosed a little boy with wanting
to kill his dad based on his fear of horses. I rode
a horse once, slipped half out of the saddle
and was dragged nearly half a mile. I laughed

at the bruises and the muddy blouse. Get out
says the gym teacher who catches me
kissing a boy behind the bleachers. The boy
laughs as he pulls me along by the waist.

It has been proven that get out was only meant
for me. I am not afraid of horses. But I think
my psychology teacher should know I have
wanted to kill before, when I heard my name

in a rumour but the boy pulled me away
from his laughing friends saying I am hearing things
where there is nothing at all. He acts like I've seen
a wolf or a butterfly but I know from class

those mean sex, what Freud knew of paranoia
in women was it could be healed by his touch.
I am sure the women who were supposed to be
his patients only wanted to tell him to fuck off.

None of the girls in class are laughing,
we've been dragged around long enough.
I think my eyes might be broken,
because my ink blot looks like a clock.

Kyla Pereles (17)

Exam Questions

I've learned to accept my life is load of problems
and half of them are still not solved, my days
everyday a car going at constant speed.

For example: Why when my father abused me
did I say we were play fighting when I still
had red marks on my back? Why

did my mum abuse her liver with chemical
substances, alcohol and drugs? I was never
in control. I was a single leaf picked off the tree.

And I only remembered *two positives repel*
when the car was finally stationary.

Hollie Peterson (16)

Appointments

The first doctor insists that my relationship
with food is to myself what a seed is to a fruit,
that my eating habits are the moon and all
my life's catastrophes are the tide. The second doctor

makes a diagnosis I can't pronounce.
My father tells me I will fuck up my life
if I don't get a grip, which is all
strictly medical terms. I want

a perfect life that everyone is jealous of.
I want all the water I touch to turn
into pearls, I want a miserable life
that everyone is jealous of.

Summer is to me
what a stained-glass window is to a fist.
I should have prefaced this poem with an apology,
to my family and to the NHS

because there is nothing you can say to a poet
and be certain it won't be set loose again.

Helen Woods (17)

One of me is writing again,

hand gripping onto words
that were not made for her,
the phrases are little more
twisted than usual, a little
more spiteful.

A younger version of me
is thinking about the cats
she doesn't have and there's a me
who only thinks about
that boy at the bus stop
the way his shoes looked
the way we looked at each other
the way he looked at me
when I wasn't looking at him.

There's a me out there who prays
the way her grandma taught her,
hands clapped together
at the bottom of the bed
she whispers something in Spanish
and then something in English
and opens her eyes and waits for miracles.

There's a me that hates my mum,
there's a me who only loves my mum.
There is a me who only reads funeral poetry.
The best version of me isn't here yet.

The other versions of me wait for her,
thinking about her at night
before they can't think any more.

She will know
that the capital of Somalia is Mogadishu
and how to wake up at 5:50 in the morning
to go on runs and
fold up her body in yoga.
She has sorted out her student finance
and remembers to take
her hayfever medication.
She travels and knows
the feeling of pillows
at 5-star hotels. She ends nights
dancing salsa with men
who are handsome professors,
a musician, a spy, a lawyer
but falls in love with none.
She is thin and thin and thin.
She is not scared of attention
and will not ever crave it.

The first me stops writing.
She reads herself back
untwisting spaghetti f's.
She crosses a line out,
and gets back to her stanza.

Aisha Borja (18)

My Teacher

(for Bernadine)

You with your old-fashioned M&S blazers,
always late to lessons with a coffee
from the cafeteria machine. Red ink on the page,

coffee stains and biting remarks, grammar
above all, God is French grammar,
war against French grammar. Kindly

forgetting that I wasn't on the list
for the school trips, knowing already
I'd changed my mind and wanted to go.

You watched my life unravel between lessons,
offered me a poem about chaos
and sent me home when I needed to go.

I see you: head of white hair, like a bob-cut halo,
hear your heels clacking down a narrow corridor,
on the way to help someone else.

Chantale Davies (18)

Grown ups

The day I run out of words for
how easy and difficult it is to hear

myself speak at dinner, I tell a story
that isn't mine, about the things my mother

believes – that if you are good at cards
you are unlucky in love, that you must always

pray for the light when it enters a
room and flush the toilet after a bad

dream, and I finish with the Nepalese proverb
that you hiccup when someone thinks

of you because lately I've been holding on
to this one like some morning prayer.

It comes on my run by the meadows
avoiding the geese, on my evening bike

ride listening to bats for the first
time, squinting at Venus. I tell the sky

it is better to hold hands with these
superstitions than with a man too

drunk to take me to school, a man
who believes that other than a scooter

there is nothing a father can give a son
who has learned to walk all alone

like a grown up.

    Mukahang Limbu (19)

To Do at Uni

You could go to to sleep at a reasonable hour
when there's much to be done,
or not; stay up for several hours,
join conversations with the lights off
watch the sunset reflected
on the post-it notes pinned to the walls,
confessionals after dark with fairy-lights
draped over your shoulders.
Then go out and hear your heels clatter on old
uneven pavements,
keeping balance then
losing it on stable ground,
be caught when you fall
and hold on when you're fine again.
And notice the moonlight
on a clock tower, learn
that night is not dark,
it's blue, it's silver, it's
a rosy gold leaking from streetlamps.
And sense the mist rising around you,
ghostly boats floating in the fog
on a canal, and let it remind you
of home, the damp, grey country air.
Count everything you missed,

but be content all the same.

Chantale Davies (18)

Today

The year was a skylark,
a dot above the frost-lined sky.
The year was a moon-shaped canvas
skulking behind the shining oil painting.
The year was a book of lined pages, empty
and fragile. The year was a pot of under-ripe
pansies, tilted away from the sun.

But this morning
smells like prime factors,
brown pine needles. Today
tastes like snow. Today is a single cloud
bobbing through blue skies. And today I am
Winter and the leopard stalking through it. I am
the frost-lined window, I am the crack of light.

Annie Davison (11)

Note

When all this is over I am planning
to meet you in a coffee shop where I'll lean way
back like a free man and hold my cup
to the air as if inspecting a jewel.

I'm hoping for rain so hard we can't tell
what are stars and which are raindrops so
we have to stand under the same black bat-like
umbrella. Looking at the halo round

the streetlamp will remind me of how
I used to be scared of the dusk sky.
I'll tell you this, quietly, as you'll be close
enough to hear me. *Where were you during*

the total eclipse, I'll ask. By the time this is over,
it'll be winter, high time for ice-skating.
We'll make music stave tracks behind us
and when I trip you'll be allowed to

reach out and catch me.

Linnet Drury (17)

What I Miss When I'm Away

The simple fact of the dog.
And the cat, who clambers on shoulders
to purr in people's ears, and who dodges,
artfully, between kitchen chairs.
My dad, who cannot sneeze quietly,
and my mum, who cries at the news.

My room, mine since I was nine,
the single bed, where I read, and sometimes slept.
The cars outside the window and
the lights on the wall as they pass.
The Wendy-house in the garden,
And the lavender. That vase.

And who I was when I was at home:
that boy, hand out, at the bus stop,
the one running through the lanes
who thought he wanted to get away
and now wants, mainly, to get back.
To walk up the path like a pilgrim.
Who prays that the door's on the latch.

Brennig Davies (20)

The Story of this Book

From 2009 to 2019, I was Writer in Residence at my local comprehensive school, Oxford Spires Academy. It was a special time in the life of the school. There was a headteacher, Sue Croft, with a whole-hearted belief in the arts, an astonishing gathering of talents in the English Department and a coming together of local communities to create an especially mixed student body. Our pupils might not have had wealth or fantastic test scores, but, as the staff liked to remind each other, they had fifty-four languages, families from every continent and social background and, with that, a hunger to learn and a warmth it would be hard to match anywhere else. Their hearts were open.

So open, in fact, it sometimes felt as if we could have told them to be anything – astronauts, acrobats or arctic explorers – and they would have obliged. As it was, through a project which grew year by year, we told them they could be poets. We wrote in class groups, during after-school and lunch-time sessions. We created special groups to include different language groups, special educational needs, boys, girls, and young people at risk. We held year-group and whole-school competitions and celebrations. We held our own festivals and attended others. All the time we were writing, we were also reading: many of the poems here are direct responses to other poems, others come from the poets' own reading, often in the special Poetry Hub in the school library. You can read more about this teaching method in my memoir, *Some Kids I Taught and What They Taught Me*, or try out some of the exercises in *How to Grow Your Own Poem*.

Poems and poets need to be read, and we found different ways of doing this. We self-published dozens of books, from individual pamphlets and class magazines to weighty whole-school anthologies. We entered and won national competitions. We made a programme for Radio 3: *We Are Writing a Poem About Home*. Then we started sharing the poems on Twitter and steadily gained a following. This had a huge effect: our young poets suddenly knew they had a real, instant audience. It gave them an incentive to take themselves seriously and to write more and better. If you are reading this book because you follow us there – thank you for your contribution.

Soon, we had so many poems that we needed a book. In 2018, we published with Picador an anthology of poems solely by our migrant and refugee pupils. *England: Poems from a School* received the kind of success we could only have dreamed of: respectful, thoughtful readings and reviews, wide sales, almost instant re-anthologizing, translations, glorious opportunities for our poets. At this time, I started to teach at the University of Reading, and found many more talented, if slightly older, poets.

In school though, my work had to wind down. Our enabling headteacher had retired, and in 2020 the pandemic finally ended all workshops. In response, and without any sponsorship, I started a poetry group online for whoever was able to join in. The isolation and long sessions favoured older, already committed students, but Covid gave us something powerful to write about, and sent even more people to the internet looking for something good to read. Zoom, we also discovered, could break down national borders; through an Arts Council workshop we gained a new member, Kyla Pereles from Chicago, and then, after workshops in Mansfield College, Oxford, Brennig Davies, from Wales. Soon, our small group of sixth formers were documenting the pandemic to a regular audience of thousands. We created an anthology about the pandemic, *Unmute*, and put it online.

The poems in this book have been gathered from all these years, groups, anthologies and experiences. There are more than thirty poets included. The age given beside the name of the poet is their age when the poem was first created, so you can observe some of them growing up. You can also read a little more about the poets, and about how their poems came to be, in the biographies below. There is a huge range, both in the backgrounds and experiences of the poets, and in their attitude to poetry. A few of them are prodigies and are making a life in writing, but many more have gone on to different projects, taking only an interest in poetry with them. As a teacher, I'm very happy with either outcome. I believe that poetry should be part of every child's entitlement in school, something to enjoy for a while and return to, or not, in adult life. I also believe that every school could be full of the sort of poetic talent displayed in this book if we only cared to look, in the same way that almost every human can sing, albeit not solo. Each poet here is an individual talent and voice in their own right, part of their school and generation, and part of a bigger conversation with each other and with poetry. We hope you feel empowered to join in.

A donation from the sale of this book will be made by Swift to Asylum Welcome (registered charity number 1092265), who offer information, advice and practical support to asylum seekers, refugees and vulnerable migrants living in Oxfordshire.

The Poets

JAMIE ALLPORT
Jamie wrote 'My Dog' in a Year 7 English lesson with Ms Hartigan's class (Toby, Edie, Alex and Nymph were in the same group) because, he said, 'I found it an escape to write about my emotions, since the paper absorbed them and kept them secret.' Jamie is now studying for A Levels.

TIMILEYIN AMUSAN
Timi arrived in the UK from Nigeria aged fifteen without a winter coat, but carrying a well-developed interest in poetry. Mukahang brought him to poetry group, and before long he was writing the poems you can read here and composing pieces for the Orchestra of St John's and the BBC. He's currently studying Construction Engineering Management at the University of Portsmouth.

MOHAMED ASSAF
Mohamed arrived in the UK as a refugee from Syria in 2016. 'Sham' is about the struggle to learn English.

ANNA BEEKMAYER
Anna started writing in Year 7 alongside Maddie, Eva, Amber, Linnet, Annie, Amaani and Ellie. She is currently finishing A Levels with a place to read Biomedical Sciences at Oxford. Her poem 'OX4' became so famous, she was even asked about it in her interview.

AISHA BORJA
Aisha is extremely dyslexic and devoted to poetry. After winning several national awards at school, she gained a place

at Queen Mary College, London. She particularly enjoys spoken-word poetry and is interested in how it reflects current political movements. She writes about those closest to her, especially her Dutch/Colombian family.

EVA BRAND WHITEHEAD
Eva was startled to win the Foyle Young Poets of the Year Award when she was just twelve. This just made her realize she had a lot of writing to do, so she kept at it through school all the way to a place to study Biology. Eva is also a remarkable runner.

JASMINE BURGESS
Jasmine started writing poetry at age eleven and won the Betjeman Poetry Prize and the Foyle Young Poets of the Year Award a year later. She is now studying Maths at Durham University, and is leading her college's LGBT+ association.

NYMPH CARTER
Nymph created their own poetry pamphlet at fourteen and is now a seventeen-year-old non-binary who enjoys writing poetry and scripts. They are currently studying theatre at a drama college in Oxford, but have continued to write poetry in their free time.

JOANNA CHAMPION
When Joanna was a teenager, school wasn't her favourite place. But she enjoyed her poetry group with Amber Day and Hollie, and won a place on an Arvon course. Fast forward to 2021 and she is a Front of House SCR Assistant at St John's College, Oxford.

Maisie Crittenden

Maisie often described herself as a future athlete rather than a scholar at school, but a struggle with disability forced her off the pitch aged fourteen. After a slight reworking of her career plans, she is now studying English at the University of Reading and thriving as both rugby player and poet.

Brennig Davies

Bren is from the small village of Wenvoe in the Vale of Glamorgan, South Wales, and writes in both Welsh and English. He hadn't written poems before coming to Kate's workshops in Mansfield College, Oxford, in 2020 but now finds it hard to stop.

Chantale Davies

Chantale is half Polish and Welsh, from a village near Swansea in South Wales. She has previously written poetry and scripts, ran a creative-writing club at her secondary school, and is currently studying at Mansfield College, Oxford.

Annie Davison

Annie's sophisticated, delicate poems have won her prizes in the Betjeman and Foyle competitions. She made a huge contribution to the *Unmute* anthology. Next year, she's hoping to study English Literature at York.

Amber Day

Amber is half Italian. She was wild at school, but always turned up for poetry group. After learning to call 999 at the age of four, Amber is very proud to be now working as a police emergency call-taker.

LINNET DRURY

Linnet's poems have been commended in the Betjeman and Tower prizes, and in 2020 won the Foyle Young Poets of the Year Award. Over lockdown, her poems were retweeted thousands of times, made into films, set for choirs and generated the hashtag *#LinnetforLaureate*. She has a place to study Maths and Philosophy at Oxford.

ALEX DUNN

Alex wrote this poem in Ms Hartigan's class while trying not to listen to the racket Nymph and Toby were creating. He is gifted in Maths and Music and is pursuing them at A Level.

AMBER FRIZZELL

Amber loves all the arts, especially writing, acting and reading. She intends to study Drama and Classics at university and pursue her passion for poetry in the future.

RACHEL GITTENS

Rachel is a very conscientious and responsible student and family member who worked particularly with Aisha and Iesha at school. Poetry allows her to put her burdens down. She writes, 'I loved doing it, because it felt so intuitively freeing, yet you could also be complex and almost sculpt your poem if you chose to.'

RHIANNA GRAHAM

Rhianna first became interested in writing her own poetry during her A Levels, when she joined Kate's creative writing club. She is now an English teacher who still enjoys writing poetry and runs her own creative writing club.

William Harrison

William came to poetry group a few times during Year 7, during which he wrote, apparently effortlessly, the startling pieces in this book. We hope he will write again one day, but he seems to be busy with exams.

Iesha Jennings

Iesha has had a passion for writing since childhood, intertwining both good and bad experiences from life into poetry. Free-spirited and passionate, poetry for her is a freedom of expression. She currently writes for leisure.

Amaani Khan

Amaani always came to poetry group since Year 7. Her poems are sparse, careful and original and received an award from the Young Muslim Writers Awards in 2017. She intends to study History at university.

Frankie Lee

Frankie is currently working for GCSEs. They write: My love of writing started at a young age, when I finished my first chapter book. The book had been about Greek gods, I think, and I found myself thinking about the way the words fit together on the page, the way they felt rolling off my tongue. When I wrote my first poem all those years later, it felt like something I had been doing all my life, and from there I never stopped.

Mukahang Limbu

Mukahang Limbu is now twenty, studying English and German at Queen's College, Oxford. He is a three-time Foyle

Young Poet, a SLAMbassador and winner of the First Story National Competition. In 2019, he was the recipient of the Outspoken Prize for Poetry. At school, Mukahang was Head Boy and a huge encourager of others' poems.

EDIE MICHAEL
Edie grew up in East Oxford and wrote poems from the beginning of primary school, often in Kate's workshops. Since moving schools for sixth form, poetry has come more naturally, and she now writes every evening in her journal.

ESME PARTRIDGE
Esme was one of the first poets Kate met at Oxford Spires, and they went on many pioneering poetry adventures together, culminating in Esme's win as a Foyle Young Poet of the Year in 2013. Esme went on to study English with Creative Writing at the University of Nottingham and got a First. She fell in love with Nottingham and still lives there, working for a non-profit organization and writing poetry.

KYLA PERELES
Kyla Pereles is a Puerto Rican poet from Oak Park, Illinois. She graduated from Oak Park and River Forest High School where she was captain of the Spoken Word Club. She plans to help other Latinx youth connect with art, while attending Grinnell College in Iowa.

HOLLIE PETERSON
Hollie Peterson was an orphan at fourteen, but continued striving through her school years and continued to do her A Levels. Despite the challenges life threw at Hollie, she

remained focused and disciplined and never lost sight of her end goal. Poetry was a way of expressing how she felt and it helped her with bereavement. She left Oxford to go back to her hometown, London, where she continues to achieve goals towards becoming a Youth Worker.

Nell Peto

Nell's poems are the product of a deeply quirky mind. She is currently working on her GCSEs and, depending on her results, is either planning to become another brick in the wall or tap into the lucrative business that is poetry.

Flora Pizey

Poetry has been a fun, experimental journey for Flora, who is a committed and gifted artist. She's currently doing A Levels.

Asima Qayyum

Asima started to write poetry when she was sixteen, when she joined a creative writing workshop led by Kate Clanchy and then decided to take it as an A Level – it's the best decision she ever made. Asima now studies Politics, Economics and Law at university, while helping Kate with editorial work and working for the Rathbones Folio Prize.

Naomi Rae

Naomi Rae was born in Oxford before moving to Cheshire later on in life. She found the Zoom poetry classes a breath of fresh air during quarantine and is very grateful for the opportunity to be around such skilful poets. She is now a university student studying Fine Art in Birmingham.

Ellie Steel
Poetry and creative-writing classes were a crucial part of Ellie's development and love for writing. She is completing A Levels and planning on studying English and Creative Writing next year.

Toby Stephenson
Toby wrote a lot of poems in Ms Hartigan's class alongside Nymph and Edie, but these days spends most of his time in bed. We live in hope of a renaissance.

Zola Tatton
Zola is another dyslexic poet who loves making pictures, through words and through drawing. She also plays jazz piano.

Maddie Wolf
Maddie started writing poetry in Year 7 and took an AS Level in Year 9. Her poems have a dark, quiet magic.

Helen Woods
Helen has read and written prodigiously since childhood. She won the Betjeman Poetry Prize aged twelve and the Foyle Young Poets of the Year Award at seventeen. She is currently at Wadham College, Oxford, reading English.

Louie Wright
'When I Was a Kid I Waited' was a huge hit on social media and has always meant a lot to Louie too. Louie still lives in Oxford, and loves and makes music.

Acknowledgements

Thank you to

The organizations who supported my work at Oxford Spires Academy: Oxford City Council, Oxford Brookes University, Oxford University Prismatic Translation, Creative Multilingualism, Oxford Inspires, The Forward Foundation and the Royal Society of Literature. Special thanks to Steven Matthews, Susannah Herbert and Matthew Reynolds.

The poets who were especially inspirational for our group, and who even visited us: Raymond Antrobus, Simon Armitage, Alan Buckley, Mary Jean Chan, Imtiaz Dharker, Amy Key, Lorraine Mariner and Rebecca Perry.

The very special teachers who supported the students in every way: Emma Bate, Helen Beech, Christine Atkinson, Linda Woodley, Rhianna Graham, Siobhan Hartigan, Andrew Archibald, Jo Dunphy, Jackie Watson, Sean Masterson. Katherine Whittington was a visionary librarian. One headteacher held us all up: Sue Croft.

My editor, Kris Doyle, and my agent, Zoë Waldie, who nursed this complex book into being with the wellbeing of the poets always at the forefront of their minds.

Asima Qayyum, editorial assistant and community-liaison extraordinaire. I would be lost without you.